The
Comanche

Charles George

KIDHAVEN
PRESS™

THOMSON
★
GALE™

San Diego • Detroit • New York • San Francisco • Cleveland
New Haven, Conn. • Waterville, Maine • London • Munich

© 2003 by KidHaven Press. KidHaven Press is an imprint of The Gale Group, Inc., a division of Thomson Learning, Inc.

KidHaven™ and Thomson Learning™ are trademarks used herein under license.

For more information, contact
KidHaven Press
27500 Drake Rd.
Farmington Hills, MI 48331-3535
Or you can visit our Internet site at http://www.gale.com

LIBRARY OF CONGRESS CATALOGING-IN-PUBLICATION DATA

George, Charles, 1949–
  The Comanche / by Charles George
    p. cm. — (The North American Indians)
Summary: Discusses the Comanche people, their customs, family, organizations, food gathering, religion, war, housing, and other aspects of daily life.
Includes bibliographical references and index.
  ISBN 0-7377-1474-3 (hardback : alk. paper)
  1. Comanche Indians—History—Juvenile literature. 2. Comanche Indians—Social life and customs—Juvenile literature. [1. Comanche Indians. 2. Indians of North America—Southwest, New. 3. Indians of North America—Great Plains.]
I. Title. II. Series.
  E99.C85 G46 2003
  978.004'9745—dc21
                                                    2002010421

Printed in China

Contents

Chapter One

The People

History knows them as the Comanche Indians, but they refer to themselves as *Numunuh*, or "People." Spanish explorers and missionaries called them *Comanche*, a term they heard from one of the Comanche's rivals, the Ute. The Ute called them *Kohmahts*, which means "Those Against Us," or "Enemies." Other **tribes** called the Comanche by other names—Snake People, *Idahi*, or *Pádoucas*.

Because the Comanche had no written language, much of their early history is unknown. They, like many other American Indians, recorded major events by telling stories, singing songs, or painting images on animal hides or on cave walls. Many of their stories and songs have been passed down through the generations, but many more have been forgotten. Because they were a **nomadic** and often warlike people throughout most of their history, many of their painted records have been lost as well.

Much of what is known of the early Comanche does not come from the Comanche themselves, but from others. Neighboring tribes, opponents in battle, Spanish missionaries and settlers, and French traders all wrote about the Comanche. Much has been learned, too, from

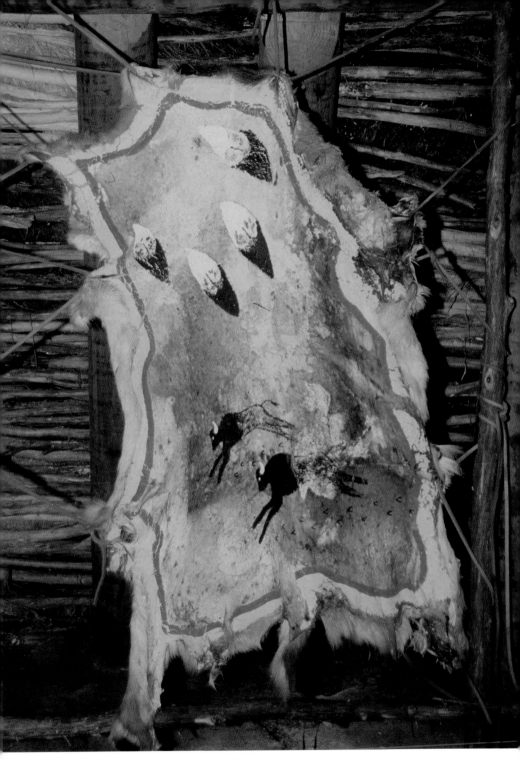

This hunting scene painted on an animal hide depicts important events in a Comanche's life.

archaeological evidence—artifacts found by scientists—and from the study of Indian languages.

Arrival of the Horse

For nearly two hundred years, this group of Native Americans controlled most of North America's southern Plains. From humble beginnings in the Rocky Mountains, the Comanche grew to be a powerful force on the Plains. For most of the eighteenth and nineteenth centuries, this nomadic group held back invaders: rival Indian tribes, then Spanish and French explorers, and finally, Anglo-American settlers. One reason for the success of the Comanche was their remarkable horsemanship.

The Comanche did not always have horses, and no one is certain exactly when they first got them. Historians do know that horses were not present in North America before Spanish **conquistadores** brought them to Mexico in the early 1500s. Later, Spanish explorers rode them northward, into what is now the United States. In 1541 Francisco Vásquez de

The Comanche were excellent horsemen, and they controlled much of the southern Plains.

Spanish conquistadors like Francisco Vásquez de Coronado first brought horses to North America. The Comanche were quick to recognize the usefulness of the animal.

Coronado led an expedition into present-day New Mexico and the Texas Panhandle. At about the same time, the expedition of another Spaniard, Hernando de Soto, entered what is now east Texas.

Horses from their herds and from other expeditions escaped, were left behind, or were traded to Native Americans. Whether running wild on the open prairie or ridden by American Indians, horses thrived on the vast grasslands of the Plains. It did not take long for Plains Indians to realize how important horses were to their survival.

From Mountain Nomads to Expert Horsemen

According to Spanish reports, the Comanche came to own horses sometime before 1714. The Comanche and the horse had a special relationship. In their language, a horse was a "god dog." All Plains Indians became good horsemen, but the Comanche were the best. The horse radically changed they way the Comanche lived.

Before the horse's arrival, the Comanche lived a relatively primitive life in the eastern Rocky Mountains. Like their ancestors, the early Shoshone, they were hunter-gatherers. They spent most of their time searching for food—small animals, berries, roots, and wild grains. They occasionally hunted larger game, such as deer or buffalo, but this was difficult on foot.

A New Way of Life

At some unknown point in their history, the Comanche split away from the Shoshone and left the mountains to wander the Plains. With the horse, their nomadic way of life became much easier. Horses allowed the Co-

Comanche warriors chase wild horses across the Plains. Owning a large herd of horses was a sign of wealth and power.

manche to move entire villages from place to place m
quickly. Horses carried heavy loads. The Comanche wc.c
able to hunt so efficiently that they had a surplus of meat
and hides for the first time in their history.

A large herd of horses was also a sign of wealth.
They could be traded to other tribes for food, tools, or
weapons. Many tribes owned herds of horses, but the
Comanche owned far more than most. In most
Comanche **bands** even ordinary warriors often owned
250 horses, and some war chiefs might have as many as
1,500. One band of two thousand Comanche was
reported to own a herd of 15,000 animals. Such wealth
and power were unheard of in other Plains tribes.

The Comanche also depended on their horses in
battle. Because of their special talent for training and
riding horses, the Comanche soon came to rule a vast
area. When other tribes tried to move in, the far superi-
or Comanche force drove them out. Warriors rode their
horses bareback (without a saddle) into battle. But even
at high speeds, they could hang off the sides of their
horses and fire arrow after arrow at their enemies. In
this way, they were shielded from harm by the bodies
of their galloping horses.

The Comanche Transformed

Off their horses, the Comanche did not resemble other
Plains Indians who were usually tall and graceful. In
contrast, the Comanche more closely resembled their
Shoshone ancestors—short, heavily muscled, and dark-
skinned. Once riding, though, they were transformed.
American artist and writer George Catlin toured the
West in the 1830s, painting hundreds of pictures of
what he observed. He also kept a detailed journal of his
experiences. In his journal he recorded how the horse
affected the Comanche.

Comanche warriors gallop bareback into battle. Their
impressive riding skills enabled them to defeat their enemies.

He wrote that Comanche warriors seemed heavy
and awkward on their feet, but once mounted, they
seemed quite different.

[The] moment they mount their horses, they . . .
surprise the spectator with the ease and elegance

of their movements. A [Comanche] on his feet is out of his element, ... as awkward as a monkey on the ground, without a limb or a branch to cling to; but the moment he lays his hand upon his horse, his *face* even becomes handsome, and he gracefully flies away like a different being.[1]

Horses allowed Comanche bands to travel quickly and easily. Here, Comanche warriors ride off as they come under attack.

In much the same way the development of steam engines and electricity changed European and American culture, the horse transformed the Comanche's. On horseback, they were no longer limited to a day's walk, or to the amount of weight they could carry on their backs. They no longer struggled daily to find food, nor worried about enemy warriors planning an attack. With the horse, the Comanche truly became lords of the Plains.

Chapter Two

The Comanchería

The territory controlled by the Comanche covered 240,000 square miles. This included most of present-day central and western Texas, eastern New Mexico, southeastern Colorado, southwestern Kansas, and all of western Oklahoma. The Comanche controlled this vast region, which was known simply as the Comanchería, the land of the Comanche.

A Sea of Grass

The land suited the nomadic lifestyle of the Comanche. A sea of grass spread before them as far as the eye could see. This part of the Great Plains is the high heartland of the North American continent. It is generally level, but broken in places by deep valleys, isolated, steep hills, and river bottoms lined with trees. Among the most striking features of the southern portion of the Great Plains are long, flat-topped ridges that rise above the prairie floor for hundreds of miles. These **escarpments** mark the edge of a seemingly endless openness called the **Llano Estacado**, or Staked Plain. This plain covers most of the Texas Panhandle and eastern New Mexico.

On the Plains, the weather was relatively mild. Summers were hot and dry, but freshwater was always nearby. In the cold winters, the Comanche knew to take shelter in the canyons or along steep hillside slopes.

The wide-open spaces of the Great Plains suited the Comanche's nomadic lifestyle.

There they would be protected from blizzards that blew across the prairies.

A Variety of Foods

Ample grass for grazing and several large rivers that cross the southern Plains made the land ideal for the Comanche's main food source—the buffalo. Some experts estimate as many as 60 million buffalo once roamed the Great Plains. Elk, deer, and antelope also lived on the Plains. Along the banks of rivers such as the Cimarron, Canadian, Washita, Red, Pease, Brazos, and Pecos, stands of cottonwood, elm, walnut, and pecan trees provided shelter, fuel, and food.

The Plains provided a surprisingly varied diet for the Comanche. Besides buffalo and other wild animals, many plants were edible. At various times of the year, Comanche women gathered and prepared wild peas, prairie turnips, wild fruits ranging from persimmons to chokecherries, milkweed buds, sweet thistle stalks, and the fruit of the prickly pear cactus.

Buffalo, shown fleeing from Comanche lances and bows, were the tribe's main food source.

The Comanche refused to eat certain foods other tribes enjoyed, even though they were plentiful on the Plains. Some tribes thought dog was a delicacy. The Comanche did not. Only extreme hunger would lead a Comanche to eat dog. The Comanche considered themselves related to the wolf. Therefore, because dogs were cousins to the wolf, the Comanche disliked eating them. They also did not eat fish, frogs, pigs, or birds because they considered them unclean. They refused to eat turkey. To the Comanche, the turkey was a coward, always running from its enemies. By eating a turkey, they feared they could become cowardly, too.

Despite endless prairie grass and the wide variety of food on the Plains, it was not always easy to find food during every season of the year. Food that could be gathered from river bottoms eventually disappeared and wild game became scarce. When this happened, the band of Comanche broke camp and moved on. Buffalo and other game migrated from place to place, depending on the season, so the Comanche followed. Home was where they camped, in canyons or in foothills, in the mountain meadows of New Mexico or out on the open prairie.

Divisions of the Comanche

The Comanche did not arrive on the southern Plains as one large, unified tribe, and they seldom united as one group. Instead they came to the Plains in small family groups or bands. Eventually more than thirteen different bands of Comanche lived in the Comanchería. Most of these were named after a food they liked, or after some other trait. The five largest were the Penateka ("Honey Eaters"), the Nokoni ("Those Who Turn Back," or "Wanderers"), the Kotsoteka ("Buffalo Eaters"), the Yamparika ("Root Eaters"), and the Quahadi ("Antelope People").

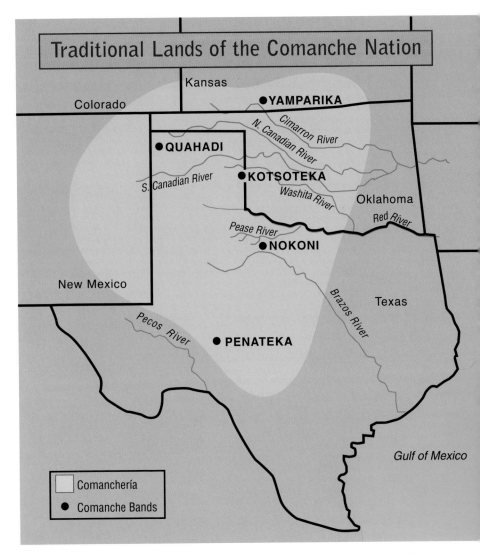

Traditional Lands of the Comanche Nation

Kansas

Colorado

● YAMPARIKA

Cimarron River

N. Canadian River

● QUAHADI

S. Canadian River

● KOTSOTEKA

Washita River

Oklahoma

Red River

Pease River

● NOKONI

New Mexico

Brazos River

Texas

Pecos River

● PENATEKA

Gulf of Mexico

☐ Comanchería
● Comanche Bands

The Penateka occupied the southernmost region of the Comanchería—along the Edwards Plateau in central Texas. Their name came from their love of honey gathered from the hives of wild bees in the area. The Penateka were among the largest and most powerful of the Comanche bands. In later years, they were the band nearest white settlements in Texas, and the ones who raided most often. They were known as the southern Comanche.

North of the Penateka, between the Brazos and Red Rivers of north-central Texas, lived the Nokoni. This band moved around more than the Penateka, seldom taking time to set up proper camps. South of the Nokoni lived a couple of smaller groups—the Tenawa ("Those Who Stay Downstream") and the Tanima ("Liver Eaters"). These three tribes were known as the middle Comanche.

From the Red River north to the Canadian River, in what is now western Oklahoma, lived seven or eight tribes that made up the Kotsoteka. All Comanche ate buffalo meat and depended on them for many of their needs, but the Kotsoteka lived near the largest herds.

Farther to the north, in what is now southwestern Kansas, lived the Yamparika. In addition to eating buffalo, they dug and ate the edible roots of the Yampa vine, as their Shoshone ancestors had done.

To the west, on the high plains of west Texas and New Mexico, lived the Quahadi. This band apparently broke away from the Kotsoteka and moved to the more isolated Llano Estacado as late as the nineteenth century. There, herds of antelope, as well as buffalo, provided meat.

By the mid-1700s about twenty-thousand Comanche were spread among the five major divisions. Some bands were large, such as the Penateka, and some, like the Quahadi, were small. For the most part, each band stayed to itself. At no time in their history did all Comanche bands come together to fight an enemy. Likewise, they never fought each other.

Tribal Organization

Although separated in some cases by hundreds of miles, all Comanche spoke the same language. They also lived basically the same lifestyle. Each followed the

Comanche bands lived in camps separate from each other, and each band kept to itself.

same rules of conduct and shared the same religious beliefs. Each band was independent, and no overall tribal organization existed. Despite this loosely organized society, their common cultural identity gave them strength and helped them stand against outsiders.

Within the various bands of Comanche, few political groups existed. No tribal leader or tribal council spoke for all the Comanche. Unlike many other American Indian tribes, the Comanche had no central chief. The only political leadership among the bands rested with the peace chiefs, the band councils, and the war chief.

Comanche peace chief Running Wolf. Peace chiefs settled arguments between band members.

Each band chose a peace chief, usually one of the eldest men. He was sometimes asked for advice, but he had no real power. His main duty was to keep the peace within the band, to help settle arguments, and to suggest solutions. A peace chief held this position of respect in the band only as long as the people listened to him and followed his advice.

All men in the band were allowed to sit on the council. Each man was allowed to speak uninterrupted in council meetings, and no decision was ever forced upon anyone. Women did not normally take part in council, but they could listen and speak if asked. Band councils usually decided such questions as when and where to move camp, whether or not to make war or peace with a neighboring tribe, when to begin large buffalo hunts, and how to divide items taken in raids and meat from hunts.

If every member of the council did not agree, the decision was delayed until more discussion could be held. If no agreement was possible, those who disagreed with the majority usually left the band to join another, or formed one of their own.

A Comanche war chief urges his men to fight. The war chief led his warriors into battle.

In times of war, the council chose the most successful and respected warrior to be war chief. This person's power was limited to whatever battle was about to be fought. During battle, the war chief led the group of warriors and organized the strategy. However, because all warriors took part voluntarily, they always had the right to leave if they disagreed with the leader. When the battle, or raid, was over, the war chief lost his power.

This system of governing may not seem efficient, but it suited the nomadic lifestyle of the Comanche. This was **democracy** in its purest sense. Every person in the band was free to speak his or her mind. Because of the vast distances that sometimes separated the various bands on the southern Plains, no form of central government could have worked as well as this one did.

Chapter Three

Daily Life on the Southern Plains

Whether following herds of buffalo or defending against invaders, moving from place to place across the Plains affected almost every aspect of the Comanche's lives. Everything they owned had to be easy to move, even their homes. Also, because some of these moves had to be made quickly, everyone had to work together as a team.

The Comanche usually camped alongside rivers or streams so they would have fresh water. Unlike some other Plains tribes, however, they did not arrange their homes in any particular order. Sometimes they put them in circles, close to other family members. At other times, they lined the banks of the stream. Larger camps stretched for miles.

Comanche Women at Work and at Play

In Comanche camps, men and women each had duties to perform. Men were responsible for hunting and protecting the village. They also participated in council meetings. Women did most of the other work—cooking, making clothing, caring for the children, and setting

Women in a Comanche village prepare buffalo hides (right), while the men of the village play a gambling game (left).

up camp. They made most of what the family needed, and much of what they needed came from the buffalo.

Comanche women dried a buffalo's stomach and intestines to use as water bags. They scraped out the horns to use as bowls, cups, and spoons. Bones became scrapers and other tools. Slivers of bone became needles for sewing. Women tanned buffalo and deer hides to make warm robes and blankets. The women also skinned and tanned the hides of rabbits, skunks, and other small animals and sewed them together for clothing. They also prepared the hides used to cover their homes.

Comanche women worked hard but were not slaves to their husbands. In fact, they had a good deal of freedom and influence over the tribe. When not working, they enjoyed playing games. The string game cat's cradle and one similar to the modern game Parcheesi, played on a decorated buffalo hide, were favorites.

Warrior Games and Weapons of War

Because women did most of the day-to-day work around camp, Comanche men enjoyed free time. They, too, liked playing games. Their games usually involved competition that used skills needed for hunting and warfare. Wrestling, foot races, archery contests, and horse races were among their favorite pastimes. They also enjoyed various forms of gambling.

The only type of camp work men did regularly was making weapons—bows, arrows, lances (spears), battle-axes, and shields. They made bows from various kinds of wood. They preferred the wood from the Osage

Making weapons, like these arrows, was a Comanche man's only regular chore around camp.

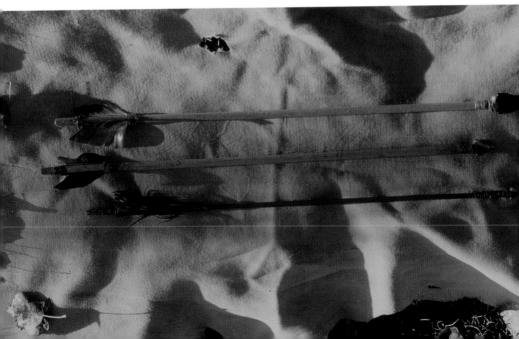

orange tree. This wood was perfect for bows because it was strong, flexible, and durable. They made the bowstring from shredded buffalo sinew (tendons), soaked in glue made from buffalo hooves. A good bow might take months to make. Comanche men usually made arrows from dogwood or mulberry wood. Wild turkey and owl feathers were glued on to make the arrows fly straight.

The most important item for a Comanche warrior in battle, other than his horse and weapons, was his war shield. To Comanche warriors, the shield was a symbol of power. Each warrior made his own shield. He used layers of the toughest buffalo hide, stretched across a wooden frame, and stuffed between with furs. A well-made shield could deflect a spear or an arrow—sometimes, even a bullet.

A Comanche's shield was more than physical protection from an enemy's weapon. In his eyes, a shield contained magical powers. Each warrior decorated his shield with images or objects he believed would aid him in battle—bear's teeth, human hair, or a horse's tail. Because of the mystical importance of his shield, a Comanche warrior would never allow others to touch it. In fact, he never brought his shield inside his home, because he worried that it might somehow lose its power.

The Comanche Tepee

Home for the Comanche was a **tepee**—a cone-shaped tent covered in buffalo hides. Comanche women could raise or lower these tepees in minutes. Each family built its tepee in much the same way. Construction began with four poles, usually pine or cedar, between ten and twenty feet long. Other Plains tribes used a base of three poles, but the Comanche, like their Shoshone ancestors, used four.

Comanche warriors made shields like this one from buffalo hide, decorating them with objects and pictures they believed would bring success in battle.

The women tied the poles together, a few feet from one end, then stood them upright, with the tied ends at the top. Then, they spread the other ends on the ground, forming a circle. Once the basic framework was erected the poles were secured into the ground. Sometimes the poles went as deep as three feet, so the tepee could withstand strong winds.

They then added eighteen other poles, tied them to the tops of the base poles, and secured them into the earth. This formed a circle on the ground about twelve to fifteen feet in diameter. Once the poles were secured, they spread ten to seventeen buffalo hides on the poles and tied them securely. They left a hole at the top to allow smoke from the tepee's campfire to

The Comanche lived in buffalo-hide tepees. Here, a Comanche on horseback guards his family's tepee.

escape. The women could adjust the size of this hole by folding or unfolding the hides. The structure's door consisted of a small opening near the base of the tepee, covered by a stiff flap of tanned buffalo hide or bearskin.

A Cozy Home

Inside the tepee, furnishings were simple. Beds made of soft piles of buffalo robes lay along the edges. Sometimes, the Comanche built raised wooden platforms, covered with rawhide strips, to get the beds off the cold ground. They kept their other possessions—food, clothes, and other personal items—in large leather pouches called **parfleches**.

Comanche women kept a small fire burning inside the tepee for warmth. Cooking was done outside, but in severely cold weather, they cooked inside. In slightly warmer weather, hides along the base of the tepee were rolled up to allow air to flow through. The Comanche lived in tepees only during colder weather. In summertime they preferred sleeping outdoors under the stars, or under **brush arbors**, open shelters covered with branches or bundles of grass.

Comanche Fashions

Animal hides not only provided shelter for the Comanche. They also provided clothing. In summertime, men wore leather belts with **breechclouts**. Breechclouts consisted of a long piece of buckskin pulled between their legs and hung from their belts, in front and back. They seldom wore anything on their upper bodies. In winter, though, Comanche men wore heavy buffalo robes around their shoulders and fur-lined buffalo-hide boots.

Comanche women also wore leather clothing, but their's was more colorful than the men's. They spent a

Comanche women usually wore deerskin outfits (center).
Comanche children rarely wore clothing.

lot of time making deerskin shirts and long skirts,
attaching long fringes of leather strips, human hair, or
animal fur, and sewing on ornate patterns of beads or
bits of metal. Children seldom wore clothing until they
were eight years old.

Both men and women wore leather leggings that ex-
tended from their belts to their moccasins. Comanche
moccasins were different from those of many other

Indian tribes. Because the Comanche spent so m
time on horseback, they made their moccasins more like
boots, with tough buffalo hides for soles, and softer deerskin on top.

Hairstyles and Headdresses

The Comanche seldom wore anything on their heads.
Women usually kept their hair short. Men took great
pride in their hair, allowing it to grow quite long. They
parted it down the middle and braided it, sometimes
covering the braids with beaver fur. Both men and
women painted their scalps along the part with yellow,
red, or white clay.

Comanche men took great pride in their long braids,
decorating them with beads, fur, and feathers.

Men also braided a strand of hair from the tops of their heads, called a scalp lock, intertwining it with colored cloth, beads, or a single feather. In battle some warriors wore a headdress made from the scalp and horns of a buffalo. By doing so, they felt they might share in the buffalo's strength and courage.

Besides providing food, shelter, and clothing, buffalo figured prominently in the Comanche religion. Other animals also played important roles, as did the earth, the sky, and other elements of nature.

Chapter Four

Strong Medicine

For people always on the move, and often at war, strength was everything. Physical strength and spiritual strength had equal importance to the Comanche,and much of this power—what they called **puha** or "medicine"—came from the spirits of certain animals.

Comanche Religious Beliefs

Unlike other Plains tribes, the Comanche did not have an organized, tribal religion. There were no priests and few religious ceremonies. Trying to understand the mysteries of life was personal for the Comanche. Each person practiced an individual religion for specific purposes.

They believed in the Great Spirit, an all-powerful creator who ruled the universe. According to one source, the Comanche believed the Great Spirit created people from many different things:

> the body from the earth, the bones from the stones, the blood from the dew, the eyes from the depth of the clear water, the beauty from his own image, the light of the eyes from the sun, the thoughts from the waterfalls, the breath from the wind, and the strength from the storms.[2]

They believed in life after death, and that the after-life was much like their lives on the Plains. They some-times called the afterlife "The Happy Hunting Ground." Therefore, they did not fear death. Free of that fear, they

Comanche boys, dressed in traditional clothing, prepare for a ceremonial dance.

sought what power they could from the world around them, through **vision quests** or dreams.

Vision Quest

Every Comanche boy, before going on his first hunt or war trail, went through a vision quest. This private ceremony was one of the most important events of his life. The youth left camp for a secluded spot. There he prayed to the spirits, perhaps smoked tobacco, sang, fasted (went without food), or inflicted pain on himself, waiting for the spirits to speak.

Whatever happened during his quest he took as a sign. If he heard a wolf howl, he might believe his spirit guide was the wolf. A bull elk, bear, mountain lion, or coyote might wander near him, and he might consider this a vision. A high wind, a storm, or a shooting star could also be his guide. These vigils sometimes lasted four days and nights. Once a young Comanche found his *puha,* it was his for the rest of his life.

The Comanche believed certain animals would appear to them, bringing signs or omens of things to come. They carefully observed the behavior of these animals to help them predict the future. A bull elk was considered a good helper when falling in love or starting a family. Bears had the power to heal. Eagles and hawks were guides in wartime. Skunks had supernatural powers. A Comanche warrior often tied a skunk's tail to his horse's tail in battle. They thought badgers, horned toads, crows, and crickets could see the future or tell them where to find buffalo herds.

The End of an Era

Throughout their history on the Plains, the Comanche's *puha* was strong. They defeated all their enemies and kept invaders out of the Comanchería. Their skills as horsemen, warriors, and hunters helped them survive. However, in the mid-1800s their life began to change. They had been successful in keeping the Spanish and Mexicans out of their territory. With the independence of Texas from Mexico in 1836, though, their way of life was never the same again.

Once Texas became independent, settlers flooded into the area from the United States. These Anglo-American settlers quickly spread from east and central Texas onto Comanche lands. Texas officials negotiated several treaties with the Comanche, but each time, Anglo settlers wanted more.

Comanche warriors surrender to the U.S. Army. Settlers in Texas forced the Comanche from their land.

After decades of Indian raids, U.S. Army attacks on Comanche villages, and treaties signed and broken, Texas and the federal government began an assault on the Plains Indians, and particularly on the Comanche. In addition, greedy American buffalo hunters took over the Plains, shooting every buffalo just for the hides. Unlike the Comanche, who used every part of the buffalo, the hunters left thousands of rotting carcasses on the Plains. Within a few years, the Comanche's main source of food and clothing had mostly disappeared. Without the buffalo, it was only a matter of time before the Comanche would have to surrender.

This surrender occurred in 1874. In a brutal military campaign, troops from Fort Sill, Oklahoma, from Fort Union, New Mexico, and from Fort Concho, Texas, pursued the Comanche across the prairies. Many bands of Comanche gave up and moved onto the reservation the government prepared for them in southwestern Oklahoma. But the Quahadi resisted.

In October 1874 troops under Colonel Ranald S. Mackenzie surprised a large group of Quahadi Comanche camped in Palo Duro Canyon, near present-day Amarillo, Texas. Mackenzie attacked, and his men set fire to the camp, destroying tepees, clothing, and food. To ensure the Quahadi's surrender, Mackenzie ordered his men to shoot more than fifteen hundred horses the fleeing Comanche had left behind. The following summer, on June 2, 1875, the last remaining free Comanche, under Chief Quanah Parker, arrived at Fort Sill.

Life on the Reservation

Once there, American officials tried to force the Comanche to give up their own culture and adopt white ways. Children were sent to church schools to learn English and become Christian. They were forbidden from

A Comanche warrior carrying a white flag of surrender meets U.S. Army officers.

practicing their own religion. Officials also tried to teach them to farm, something the Comanche had never done. Conditions on the reservation were almost unbearable, but the Comanche, and their *puha,* remained strong. They survived.

Today, according to the U.S. Census, there are twelve thousand Comanche in the United States. About half of them live near the tribal headquarters near Lawton, Oklahoma. Many others live in Texas, New Mexico, and California. The Comanche Nation today has its own constitution, its own local government, and its own schools. Each year, the Comanche participate in numerous local **powwows**, especially the Comanche Homecoming Powwow, held each July in Walters, Oklahoma.

In 1867, eight years before the end of Comanche rule on the Plains, Chief Ten Bears, of the Yamparika band, spoke for his people at Medicine Lodge Creek in Kansas. In his speech, he spoke clearly and simply about his people's lost way of life:

> You have said that you want to put us on a reservation, to build us houses and make us medicine lodges. I do not want them. I was born under the prairie, where the wind blew free and there was nothing to break the light of the sun. I was born there where there were no enclosures and everything drew a free breath. I want to die there and not within walls. I know every stream and every wood between the Rio Grande and the Arkansas. I have hunted and lived over that country. I live like my fathers before me and like them I lived happily.[3]

Notes

Chapter One: The People

1. Quoted in Walter Prescott Webb, *The Great Plains.* Boston: Ginn, 1972, p. 65.

Chapter Four: Strong Medicine

2. Ernest Wallace and E. Adamson Hoebel, *The Comanches: Lords of the South Plains.* Norman: University of Oklahoma Press, 1986, p. 193.
3. Quoted in T.R. Fehrenbach, *Comanches: The Destruction of a People.* Cambridge, MA: Da Capo Press, 1994, p. 476.

Glossary

bands: Loosely organized groups of people, sometimes related to each other, who live and travel together.

breechclouts: Soft pieces of hide or cloth, usually worn by American Indian men, wrapped between the legs and held in place by a belt or string around the waist.

brush arbors: Simple, open-air shelters, made of a raised wooden platform and covered with branches, vines, or bundles of grass for shade.

conquistador: Spanish term for "conqueror," usually associated with Spanish soldiers who accompanied early explorers of the New World.

democracy: A system in which every member has equal power.

escarpments: Long cliffs or steep slopes separating two relatively level or gently sloping surfaces.

Llano Estacado (Staked Plain): A vast, flat region in eastern New Mexico and northwestern Texas that some say got its name from the stakelike yucca plants that dot its surface.

nomadic: Roaming about from place to place.

parfleches: Folded leather pouches used by American Indians for storing dried foods, clothing, or blankets.

powwow: An American Indian social gathering, usually with ceremonial dancing, singing, games, and feasts.

puha: Comanche word for "medicine," the magical power American Indians felt came from nature.

tepee: A cone-shaped, portable shelter made from poles and buffalo hides or canvas.

tribes: Organized groups of people whose members share common ancestors, culture, language, or religion.

vision quests: Solitary ceremonies practiced by American Indian boys upon reaching a certain age. The purpose is to obtain spiritual power from something in nature, such as animals or weather.

For Further Exploration

Nonfiction

Judith Alter, *Comanches.* Danbury, CT: Franklin Watts, 1994. A simple introduction to the Comanche, their history, lifestyle, and current situation.

Raymond Bial, *The Comanche.* Tarrytown, NY: Benchmark Books, 2000. An extensively researched book examining the history, cultural beliefs, and "lifeways" (dress, handicrafts, food, and games) of the Comanche. Comanche recipes are also provided.

Richard M. Gaines, *Comanche.* Edina, MN: Checkerboard Library, 2001. Full-color illustrations and easy-to-read text cover such topics as crafts, family life, myths, and important members of the Comanche tribe.

Sally Lodge, *The Comanche.* Vero Beach, FL: Rourke, 1992. Examines the history, lifestyle, and current situation of the Comanche.

Bill Lund, *The Comanche Indians.* Mankato, MN: Bridgestone Books, 1997. An overview of the past and present lives of the Comanche, covering daily life, customs, and the Comanche's relationship with the U.S. government and others. Includes maps, a hands-on activity, and full-color illustrations.

Martin J. Mooney, *The Comanche Indians.* Broomall, PA: Chelsea House, 1993. A clearly written, well-organized introduction to the Comanche.

Fiction

Joyce Eseley, *Shining Star.* Unionville, NY: Royal Fireworks Press, 1995. The fictional story of a ten-year-old Comanche girl. Extensively researched, with a great deal of accurate information about Comanche customs and activities, including tepee making and moving, foods and diet, buffalo hunting, horse raids, arrow making, tanning hides, courtship, and more.

Janice Shefelman, *Comanche Song.* Austin, TX: Eakin Press, 2000. Fictionalized account of events surrounding two major historical events in Comanche history (Council House Massacre and Battle of Plum Creek) as told through the eyes of a sixteen-year-old Comanche boy. Contains a glossary of Comanche and Spanish terms. On the New York Public Library's 2001 list of Best Books for the Teen Age.

Websites

The Comanche Language and Cultural Preservation Committee (www.comanchelanguage.org). A great site for learning about the Comanche, their history, and their language.

Comanche Nation: Lords of the Plains (www.comanchenation.com). Home page for the Comanche Nation in Oklahoma. Information can also be obtained by writing: Comanche Nation, PO Box 908, Lawton, OK 73502.

Numuukahni/Comanche Lodge (www.comanchelodge.com). Another good site devoted to the Comanche. Contains a lot of information about the tribe today.

Texas Indians (www.texasindians.com). Extensive information about tribes and languages, with many photos, maps, activities (such as making dioramas, masks, etc.), and American Indian recipes. Also provides curriculum materials and information for teachers and parents.

Index

Picture Credits

Cover: Denver Public Library, Western History
    Department.
© Bettmann/CORBIS, 7
© Historical Picture Archive/CORBIS, 14
© Mary Evans Picture Library, 8, 19
© Brandy Noon, 17
© Smithsonian American Art Museum, Washington, DC/
    Art Resource, NY, 6, 10, 11, 15, 20, 21, 24, 28, 30, 31, 36,
    38
© Marilyn "Angel" Wynn/nativestock.com, 5, 25, 27, 34

About the Author

Charles George taught history and Spanish in Texas public schools for fifteen years. He now lives with his wife, Linda, in the mountains of south-central New Mexico. Together, they have written more than forty young adult and children's nonfiction books during the past few years. Charles has written two Lucent books, *Life Under the Jim Crow Laws* and *Civil Rights*, and the KidHaven book *The Holocaust*. He and Linda also wrote *Texas*.